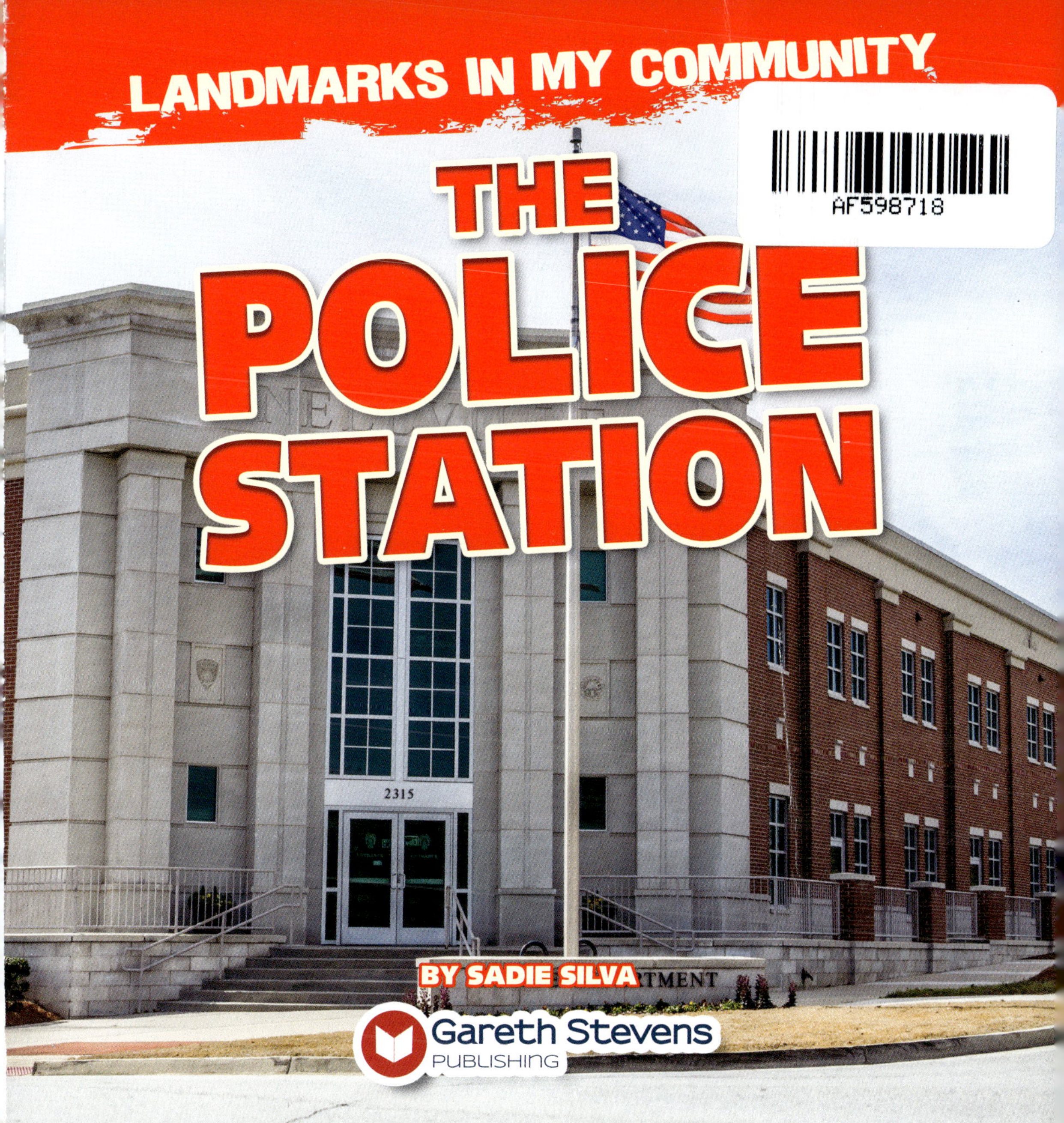

LANDMARKS IN MY COMMUNITY

THE POLICE STATION

BY SADIE SILVA

Gareth Stevens PUBLISHING

Please visit our website, www.garethstevens.com. For a free color catalog of all our high-quality books, call toll free 1-800-542-2595 or fax 1-877-542-2596.

Library of Congress Cataloging-in-Publication Data
Names: Silva, Sadie, author.
Title: The police station / Sadie Silva.
Description: Buffalo, NY : Gareth Stevens, [2025] | Series: Landmarks in my community | Includes index.
Identifiers: LCCN 2023034799 (print) | LCCN 2023034800 (ebook) | ISBN 9781538293195 (library binding) | ISBN 9781538293188 (paperback) | ISBN 9781538293201 (ebook)
Subjects: LCSH: Police–Juvenile literature.
Classification: LCC HV7922 .S526 2025 (print) | LCC HV7922 (ebook) | DDC 363.2–dc23/eng/20230811
LC record available at https://lccn.loc.gov/2023034799
LC ebook record available at https://lccn.loc.gov/2023034800

Published in 2025 by
Gareth Stevens Publishing
2544 Clinton Street
Buffalo, NY 14224

Designer: Andrea Davison-Bartolotta
Editor: Caitie McAneney

Photo credits: Cover, p. 1 The Brownfowl collection/Shutterstock.com; series art (page numbers) art_of_sun/Shutterstock.com; series art (map background) Marian Salabai/Shutterstock.com; p. 5 Motortion Films/Shutterstock.com; p. 7 BCFC/Shutterstock.com; p. 9 woodsnorthphoto/Shutterstock.com; p. 11 Ground Picture/Shutterstock.com; p. 13 John Roman Images/Shutterstock.com; p. 15 PeopleImages.com - Yuri A/Shutterstock.com; p. 17 Billy F Blume Jr/Shutterstock.com; p. 19 PL Gould/Shutterstock.com; p. 21 (background) TFoxFoto/Shutterstock.com; p. 21 (people) Sean Locke Photography/Shutterstock.com.

Printed in the United States of America

CPSIA compliance information: Batch #CS25GS: For further information contact Gareth Stevens, New York, New York at 1-800-542-2595.

CONTENTS

Boldface words appear in the glossary.

Community Helpers

If you have an **emergency**, who do you call? You would call 911, which would **connect** you to community helpers. Many times, police **respond** to emergency calls. They are at the police station or in their police cars, ready to help.

1028
POLICE
POLICE

What's a Police Station?

A police station is a building where police officers work. They have offices there. They also keep their police gear there. Police cars are parked at the police station when they're not being used.

Serving Our Community
POLICE

Police stations look different in different communities. Big communities may have big police stations with many officers. They may have rooms for talking to **suspects**. They may have cells to hold suspects too. Smaller communities might have smaller police stations.

RESERVED FOR
HANDICAPPED
POLICE
DEPARTMENT
9

Who Goes There?

Some parts of a police station are **off-limits** to the public. However, people in a community can go to a police station if they find something that someone lost. They can also go there to put in a **police report**.

Who Works There?

Police officers work at police stations. Police dogs do too! Some officers work in the police station, while others drive around. Their job is to keep people safe and make sure people are following laws, or the rules of a town, city, or country.

K-9
K9

At the Police Station

A lot happens at a police station each day! Police officers read and write reports. They get calls about emergencies, such as car crashes. Some leave the police station to go to schools and teach kids about safety.

POLICE

Important to the Community

Police stations are important places in a community. They help police officers do their job to keep the community safe. They are places where people can go when they have a problem or emergency.

POLICE DEPARTMENT
506
K-9 UNIT
POLICE
K-1
POLICE
IN GOD WE TRUST
S-1
PUBLIC SAFETY

If there wasn't a police station in each community, it might take police longer to respond to emergency calls. They wouldn't have their police cars and gear close by. Some communities need big police **departments**, while others just need a few officers.

SUBWAY
SUBWAY

Your Community Police Station

Do you know where the police station is in your community? Ask your parent or teacher where it is. Is it big or small? Who works there? If a police officer visits your school, ask them questions about their job and where they work.

GLOSSARY

connect: To join together.

department: A part of a larger organization, such as a government.

emergency: An unexpected situation that needs quick attention.

off-limits: Not to be entered.

police report: A record of something thought to be unlawful.

respond: To react or reply.

suspect: A person believed to have committed a crime.

FOR MORE INFORMATION

BOOKS

Bender, Douglas. *Police Officer.* New York, NY: Crabtree Publishing Company, 2022.

Dolbear, Emily J. *Police Officers on the Scene.* Mankato, MN: The Child's World, 2022.

WEBSITES

Police
kids.britannica.com/kids/article/police/400150
Learn more about the jobs of police officers.

Police Dogs—Saving Lives
easyscienceforkids.com/all-about-police-dogs/
Learn more about dogs on the police force!

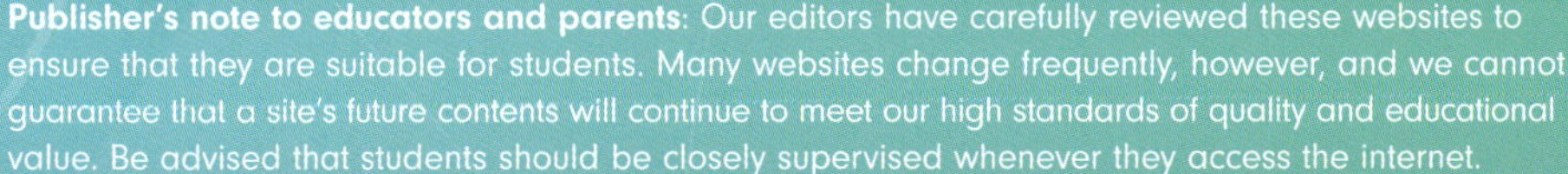

Publisher's note to educators and parents: Our editors have carefully reviewed these websites to ensure that they are suitable for students. Many websites change frequently, however, and we cannot guarantee that a site's future contents will continue to meet our high standards of quality and educational value. Be advised that students should be closely supervised whenever they access the internet.

INDEX